GW00976053

In These Places…
…At These Times

with all good wishes

Peter Thorogood

Peter Thorogood in 1955

In These Places...
...At These Times

Selected Poems
1950-1975
with illustrations by the author

Peter Thorogood

The Bramber Press

In affectionate memory of
Thelma
*for her encouragement of my writings
during a long and valued friendship*

The Bramber Press

Published by
The Bramber Press
St. Mary's House,
Bramber, West Sussex, BN44 3WE
Tel: 01903 816205

© 1997 Peter Thorogood
All rights reserved

ISBN 0 9526786 1 6

Title page:
Portrait sketch of Peter Thorogood at the piano, by Christopher Hobbs, 1968

Cover design and title page by Tony Ketteman

Typeset and printed in Great Britain by
smallprint
35 Silver Birches, Haywards Heath, West Sussex RH16 3PD

Preface

In These Places, At These Times is a representative selection of my poetry and humorous verse that covers the first thirty years of my life. The poems were composed between 1950 and 1975 and conform as nearly as possible to Wordsworth's requirement of "emotion recollected in tranquillity". If poetry is the quintessence of thought and feeling, then the impressions and memories in this small volume will reveal an unashamedly lyrical poet.

Although I have chosen traditional form and metre, I have frequently kicked over the traces in favour of free verse, though no verse is ever really 'free'. Other poems are defiantly lyrical – the radical in me refused to give in to the fashion of the day – while some are restrained in style and imagery, following Verlaine's idea that, beyond the mere words of a poem, in the blank spaces between the lines, the reader may perceive some unexpressed truth, where the poet has chosen to retain some private and precious part of his inner self.

My poetry is often unequivocally nostalgic. My roots lie in the soil of East Anglia, in the meadows and woodlands of Essex, where my father farmed the land of our ancestors. I had, however, being the youngest in the family, to set forth into the wider world of work and travel; but always, fixed in my consciousness, were images of England – memories of harvest-time and seaside holidays, family Christmases and the ever-changing English skies. Father's early death brought an end to our happy life at Albyn's Farm. My poems and water-colours from that time are a kind of affirmation, a keeping faith with the past.

If these poems prove to be, in T. S. Eliot's words, 'an easy commerce of the old and the new', I will be well-satisfied.

Peter Thorogood
St. Mary's, Bramber
June 1997

In These Places, At These Times

is a limited edition of 1000 copies of which
the first 350 are signed by the author

Number: ....

Other writings by Peter Thorogood

Poetry

The Suite of Mirrors: Translations and Elaborations from Lorca (in Home and Away, British Council, December 1967).

Love, said the Astronomers (Autolycus Press 1971).

The Once-Contented Land (Autolycus Press 1972).

Five poems in Words by Any Other Name (ed. John Bishop, Autolycus Press 1972).

Prodigal Son (Autolycus Press 1977).

Comic and Humorous Verse

A Sent-to-Coventry Carol: Verses about Men, Women and Other Beasts (Autolycus Press 1972).

Literary, Biographical, Historical

The Spoken Word (Articles for The Listener, BBC 1966-7).

English Humorous Writing (Series of broadcasts for BBC World Service 1967).

Thomas Hood and 'The Progress of Cant': A Study in Iconography (Polytechnic of Central London 1976).

Thomas Hood: A Nineteenth-century Author and his Relations with the Book Trade to 1835 (in Development of the English Book Trade 1700-1899; ed. Robin Myers and Michael Harris 1981).

Thomas Hood: Poems Comic and Serious (The Bramber Press 1995).

St. Mary's: A Home and its History (in Bramber: Glimpses of a Village, ed. Alison Noble; Beeding and Bramber Local History Society 1996).

St. Mary's Bramber: An Illustrated Guide (English Life, for The Bramber Press 1997).

Miscellaneous articles from 1991 in The Waynflete Chronicle (Journal of St. Mary's House, Bramber), on aspects of heritage and family history.

Contents

An Essex Childhood
1927-45

Carollings of Delight
1945-55

Innocence and Experience
1946-56

The Parting of the Ways
1959-72

In These Places, At These Times
1952-71

In Lighter Vein
1971

Under English Skies
1965-72

Riviera Diary
1971

Watercolours by Peter Thorogood

Front cover (top to bottom):

Cornfield Towards the Woods. Albyns Farm 1942
Summer Storm 1953
In Countryside Waking. Albyns Farm 1953
Our Village. Essex 1953

Facing page

An Essex Childhood

1927-45

At Early Light

Brightness before
The dawn is deceptive
To those who admire
Red-tinted cloud.

Over the hillsides,
Over the oceans,
Morning is wreathed
In a purple shroud.

A Boy's Song of Countryside Waking

Ghosts of silvery cloud across,
Across the shadowy indigo night,
Over spectral rings of the moon,
Veiling distant stars in flight.

Frost-hollows harbour chill of dawn,
Dawn when foxes prowl alone,
Yawning cockerel fluffs his feathers,
Farm-boys, stirring, stretch and groan.

Threshers come with chugging engines,
Engines of green, with gleaming brass;
Bullocks bellow for their breakfast,
Lazy cows roam out to grass.

Here is countryside awaking,
Waking through the mist of dawn;
Here is nature in the making:
Sunrise flowers; the day is born.

Warning to Children

                smoke
                  of
                 bon-
                fires
                curl-
                 ing
               twirl-
             ing
             over
             tree-
                tops
                creep-
                    ing
                  seep-
                  ing
             through
            windows
         flames
       flicking
       licking
        sticks and
          firewood
           lighting
             frighting
              children's
               faces glowing
              knowing scarcely
          why they do it
        who it was in
      dark November
     warmed his hands
    on glowing ember
  with explosive
 blowing sky
  high wheels of crimson
    azure comets, glittering heaven
       showering stars in brilliant clusters
            while on earth, the squibs are skipping
                  tripping on from heel to heel
              sparklers spit and flit like fireflies
            helpless guy burns bright, more brightly
             sprightly dressed in father's suit
                mute in mother's blouse and slippers:
                a child lies wounded by these joys –
             boys delight in dangerous toys.

Estuary of Thames

Russet-sailed barges roam
Seas, slicing through waves,
Wild-lurching, wind-tossed,
Bows reaching to azure dome
Of sky, a three-mile splay
Of estuary, horizon lost
In infinity of blue, bows
Plunging through a fount of spray.

Squawking gulls swoop close
Against the prancing mast,
Stunned by the gale's grip
And angry, unthwarted blast;
Bows rise out of resilient seas,
Sky drops below estuary and earth,
Making the ship's horizon
The thrusting bow-sprit's girth.

Here in these Essex waters
I made my childhood's way,
In wonderment of wave-sound,
Near to fields of home.
Swooping skyward, falling seaward,
Fleeting over foam,
Wave-loud I wandered then,
Where red-sailed barges roam.

Pastoral
1940

I can remember — leaning over a gate
and watching snakeskins drying in the breeze

I can remember dozing in a field of corn
and listening to the conversation of the trees

I can remember — clawing with my nails
and praying as the shrapnel singed my flesh

I can remember drifting in a stream
and dragging my feet in a silver quicksand mesh

I can remember — picking rosemary and thyme
and blackberrying in a warm September

I can remember — when I was a boy — deciding
how important it is to live, to feel, and to remember

On Weathering Storms
Written on the Thirtieth Anniversary of the Battle of Britain

There is no thunder
from this silver-dappled sky
though fierce flashes of light
illuminate the woods.
Black shapes begin to worry
the darkening horizon.
(Trouble travels faster
than its dull and distant thunder.)
There is such space
between earth and cloud.

Childhood memories of war intrude:
cringing and cramped, we shivered
in our waterlogged shelter,
among small green garden frogs,
a tortoise, three scowling cats,
a pet duck and a whimpering dog.
Unlike the wounded mare in the meadow,
they could not give a meaning
to that thunder. For us, bombs,
like storms, were to be expected.

Now, too, there is conflict in the skies:
the belly of cloud brushes roughly
over the low stream from the west.
A chaos of cloud blots out the sun.
Sparks split the skies.
Rain-cloud looms thunderously
over the trembling land.
Furrows are rivulets of rain;
water-meadows a rising flood.
There is no avoiding this wrath.

When all is over,
gardens are a waste land
of tangled leaf and stalk.
They will sort themselves out by morning,
now the brunt of the storm is broken.
We have known other moments like this:
As with those in war
who conquered pain or fear,
there was fresh beauty
when the storm had passed.

The Innocent Dream

When I was a child, I lived content
   Beside a silent stream.
I passed my days in quiet pursuits.
   Life was an innocent dream.
I lay in sunlit fields of corn,
   Beneath a cloudless sky.
My days were blessed with love and joy.
   I did not want to die.

Our peace was broken by alarms,
   The war took many lives,
And brave men wept to leave behind
   Their sweethearts and their wives.
I was too young to understand
   The reason for the flaw.
I asked why they should pointless die.
   They answered: "It's the war!"

We have, since then, seen many wars,
   And many millions dead.
From East to West the world is crazed.
   We live in fear and dread,
For one day soon we may wake up
   To find the world's not there —
A hole in space — where Earth had been —
   Filled in with freezing air.

When I was a child, I lived content
   Beneath a cloudless sky.
My days were blessed with love and joy.
   I did not want to die.
And now in middle years I strive
   To find that hidden stream,
Where Love lies waiting to be freed
   And peace makes real our dream.

Self-portrait (original sketch 1940, watercolour 1944)

The Fives Court, Brentwood School 1945

In the Garden of Roden House, Brentwood School 1945

Prodigal Son

The day I discovered dreaming was not enough
I felt shy and strange, and, creeping out early,
sought answers in the shining stream,
built my hide-out, like a castle, in the woodland trees,
rode the broad-backed mare at evening
to her sleepy haven in the water-meadows.

The day I discovered dreaming was not enough
I saw the white stallion glowing in the dark.
With quickening pulse, I stalked the moonshine,
lay spread-eagled on haystacks under stars,
and no-one knew I was there; but always
reality slipped through my arms.

The day I discovered dreaming was not enough,
I heard them say: "He's not the brightest boy
nor the most ignorant in our family —"
I, a stranger, yet who needed to belong,
escaped the gathering of the harvest,
was a dreamer, therefore considered odd.

The day I discovered dreaming was not enough
I was caught stealing apples (not real apples),
fell like Adam from my castle in the trees
(not a real castle of course, not of leaves),
and was drowned in the shining stream,
though not really drowned, you understand.

The day I discovered dreaming was not enough,
I packed my case and left home for the city,
where I found many people who were not farmers;
they said I was not the brightest of their friends,
neither was I the most ignorant.
They showed me another kind of harvest!

The day I discovered dreaming was not enough,
I felt shy and strange. But now I hear,
somewhere inside me, a small voice saying:
Go back. This city is not real, you understand;
we must not seek reality in dreams;
our dreams aside, reality seeks us.

Pictures in the Sand

Time in the sand. A hazy vision reigns
To conjure up faint memories of years
Spent breathing patterns on the window-panes
    Of illuminated piers.

Watch now. Catch fancy as it flies;
In lone remembrance pass away the time;
Clasp tight the mystery of childhood as it dies
    In the smart of iodine.

Fly out your streamers on the salty breeze;
Buy candy-floss and jellied eels and rock;
Spy through the telescope at distant seas;
    Hear Punch and Judy's knock.

Go on. Breathe out reflections in the sand;
Make blurred dominions clarify and glow;
Pick out the grains from tangled seaweed strands,
    Where seadrifts blow.

See in this silicate of sorrow childhood's joy,
Where now the fingertips of age are curled;
Seek out the wrinkled oyster, like a toy,
    In this dim, remembered world.

Carollings of Delight

1945-55

Peace Carol

Was there once a manger?
Was there once a star?
Were there once some shepherds?
Did they journey far?

Was there once a city
With domes as white as snow?
Was there once a holy light
That hallowed all below?

Was there once a homeland
Of truth and peace and love,
Where war and hate and cruelty
Were conquered by a Dove?

Yes, there was a time when
Stars shone clear and bright,
And led Wise Men and Shepherds
To an inn that holy night.

They could not know the meaning
Nor choose the easy way,
Their faith lay in the lonely star
That shone as bright as day.

Only Love will ease us,
Keep us safe from harm.
Let's sing our Song of Peace, now,
In anthem, hymn and psalm.

January Songs

1. Images of Janus

Father of Morning,
Ruler of Dawn,
Warden of Being,
King of New-born.

Lord of all Commerce,
Master of None,
God of the Doorway,
Prince of the Sun.

2. Song for the New Year

Old Janus is a two-faced god;
He sits astride the years;
He gazes on a year of hope,
And back on pain and tears.

So let us sing to peace and love,
Make miracles in the skies,
Melt down the riches of the earth,
And build our paradise.

The Robin and the Nightingale

Robin! here I sing your praise,
Bright muse of our bleak winter days.

Deep in dark woods, one winter night,
In this grim world of grief and folly,
I heard the cry of a lonely bird,
Among sharp leaves of winter holly.

When morning came, I found the place,
I saw the crimson berries bright,
The stain of Calvary on his breast,
His song, a carolling of delight.

Robin! here I sing your praise,
Bright muse of our bleak winter days.

Now Spring is here, and love is here,
And over primrose banks I've heard,
In sweet and plaintive descant clear,
Another song, another bird.

The nightingale rests on the thorn
And sings his heart and soul away,
Till all our sorrow's soothed with joy.
From sonorous night to rapturous day!

Nightingale! I sing your praise,
Sweet, gentle muse of April days.

For Betty Roe

The Music Tree

I have made my tree a singing tree
whose every leaf is a note,
every branch a melody,
and every blossom a song.

Though I have read of its magic,
though I have mused on its charms,
I have never seen it or heard it
even in my dreams.

I know of the trees of the sun and the moon,
the talking trees of the East,
the enchanted tree that grew by the tomb
of the incomparable singer Tan-Sein.

I have searched all my life
for a suitable song,
but my words are effigies of stone,
my thoughts unsculpted clay.

So I've made my theme the singing-tree
whose every leaf is a note,
every branch a melody,
and every blossom a song.

Innocence and Experience–
1946-56

A Song of Innocence and Experience

A unicorn drew close to me
    When I was very young,
His hide so white and smooth to touch
    And nectar on his tongue.

Young Love crept through the stable-door,
    Her skin so soft and sleek;
I kissed her and awoke to find
    The stubble on my cheek.

My unicorn became a goat,
    A shaggy hair his hide,
And I grew up a man to know
    The child in me had died.

Snake

We swam naked in the stream,
drifting in green waters,
quivering in the summer sun.
Joy was a pale word
for such ecstasy.

How vulnerable I was
when the watchful serpent
came curving towards me on the tide,
rippling and writhing
towards my nakedness.

My legs thrashed the waters.
Fleeing trout sped to the silent glooms.
Disgust seeped through my bones
as smooth green skin
brushed past my trembling throat.

What was it that made you unafraid?
Afterwards, lying on the soft bank,
I was apprehensive when this snake
crept lovingly over your shoulder
and you showed no fear.

Lines from Letters to Elizabeth

1. Promenade—
Milan, 1956

Are you thinking of me as you climb
among the castled hills of Monferrato,
in green and rose of medieval stone,
while Castor, lying close, and Pollux,
smile and doze and smile away the time?

You see what happens now, as I walk home
alone along the old Naviglio way!

I think up old rhymes and pertinent phrases;
I dream them in your dark and restless eyes,
here in the sleeping city,
under these sombre skies.

2. Sombre Serenade—
Santa Margherita, 1957

Sea, and sun, and warm sand …
Below the castle, we spoke of love
as if it were infinity.

Now, here, these wintry walls
tremble, like my heart,
in the cold cradle of your indifference;

and our old infinite —
a memory of warm sand and palms —
is pushing us apart again.

Here, by the grey impassive sea,
ours is a pointless encounter —
incontro inutile you called it.

Sun and sea, like my thoughts,
are dark with storm-clouds,
and your smile fills me with loneliness.

3. The Telephone Call
Rome, 1957

Fearing to break my news,
searching for the tender words,
I heard only your own,
like driven nails piercing
the fretted structure of the past.

Putting down the receiver
there seemed a thousand paths to follow.

4. Nocturne
Venice, 1958

These things
you have bequeathed to me now
to trouble my restless dreams.

The night is a purple splendour,
the stream is a sheen of silver,
our gondola glowing with lanterns.

Stars of gold hang in the water,
guitar music soothes in serenades,
blossom glistens over palace walls.

These things
you have bequeathed to me now
and all is folly to the world.

Trees

An Elaboration from Lorca

Green is the tree and dry is the leaf.
Fickle the heart and brittle the grief.

The girl with the dark and wistful eyes
Gathered up her olives in haste.
And the wind, the lover of turrets and towers,
Grasped her lovingly by the waist.

Four *caballeros* passed by,
On their Andalusian mules,
Dressed two in blue and two in green,
And mantles embroidered with jewels.
'O come to Cordoba with us, sweet girl.
Come to Cordoba with us.'
But she did not listen to them.

Three *torerillos* passed by,
With waists as slender as reeds,
Wearing coats of orange and silver brocade,
And silver swords born of ancient deeds.
'O come to Sevilla with us, darling girl.
Come to Sevilla with us.'
But she did not listen to them.

As evening dimmed into sepia,
And dusk in the groves diffused,
A handsome boy came courting her,
Bringing roses, moon-myrtles, and yews.
'O come to Granada with me, my love.
Come to Granada with me.'
But she did not listen to him.

The girl with the dark and wistful eyes
Gathered up her olives in haste.
And the wind, with its cold grey encircling arms,
Gripped her icily by the waist.

Green is the tree and dry is the leaf.
Fickle the heart and brittle the grief.

The Parting of the Ways
1959-72

On Leaving Home for the First Time

It was not
the journey
that hurt,
only
the departure;
first,
the tearful face,
next,
the faltering step,
then —
the great leap,
forward
into space.

It was
a long journey,
unwillingly
taken;
fear —
the uncertain path;
love —
broken by distance;
yes ...
a long journey,
unwillingly
taken,
and the price
was pain
in pleasures
I could not
awaken.

The journey
was not
about space
or time,
not of
beginning,
still less
about end;
only the love
and the knowledge
remain
to question,
unanswered,
the loss
or the gain.

Father at the Chapel of Rest

What promptings lead me to these words,
these thoughts and images
of the once-contented years?
Your tapestry of life seems rough, unfinished work,
the tangled threads reveal no sense or meaning.

You — who gave me life, paid the price,
went unrewarded, sacrificed your needs,
you — whom I had never and yet always known,
always leaned on, never thought would die,
as strangers we were, as strangers are we now.

Yet, here, where substance is the shadow,
I leap up to your dark god;
my timid heart breaks loose,
as cataracts of memory blur, inundate
this place and hour in centuries of silence.

Do you now admire the deftness of design,
the line and colour of your handiwork?
What lies beyond the experience?
Why are my thoughts dying on my lips?
Are questions all that remain
of those tender times, the long-remembered years?

One final act can heal the breach between us,
one kiss can seal the bond that makes us free.
In this my grieving, these my hopeless tears,
I make amends for all I could not be.

Eviction

1.

I remember
the anguish of watching the bailiff
silently tick his list of items,
the removal men carrying away for the last time
the memories of years,
the dreaded yet the longed-for years.

I remember
the effort of clearing
the debris of a lifetime,
of packing up the tea-chests in the hall,
of leaving a smooth clean floor
for a new tenant to walk on.

2.

I remember
the urgency of wanting
everything neatly tied up,
of getting the life-insurance
properly in order, the will
adequately signed and witnessed.

I remember
the almoner putting a mark against my name,
the immaculate nurse bringing me
my neatly-folded clothes, the surgeon
dismissing me with a smile. Apprehensive,
I walked out into the sun
clutching the new lease
nervously in my hand.

Mother in her Sickness

White clouds drift over the black moon,
sharpening the dull edge of fear,
creating from the jagged jig-saw of your life
the confused apocrypha of dreams.

On the white ceiling
you sketched in your mind's eye
a small house with a neatly-planted garden
to store your memories in, and piece together
the imperfections of the years.

Now you break the chain
with this alarming spasm of the brain
which turns your bed into a rolling ship,
speeds heart and mind
in one vertiginous flight,
changing the solid shrines of the past
into the crumbling temples
of this terror-tormented night.

Survival after pain must be,
to we who helplessly look on,
a healing miracle of flesh and soul
not written in the surgeon's notes.
Now we need more than faith
to make this hope survive.

As death bursts like a flower
into the kingdom of wondrous dreams,
believe there is something still
to show the untrodden path,
the dark tower with its sentinels,
the mysterious road we tread that twists
and winds over the distant unfamiliar hills,
and the Stranger we seem to know
silently pointing the way.

Nature Morte

this is not how I remember you

a handful of dried flowers
from your garden
sallow and lifeless

this is not how I remember you

these ears of barley
from a Normandy field
brittle and hard

this is not how I remember you

these Everlasting Flowers
(what irony of name!)
sharp and unyielding

this is not how I remember you

Venus

On Venus, the day
is longer
than the year.

Time is, like God,
beyond the bounds
of earth.

Love could be taught
to conquer
hate and fear.

Death could be just
another name
for birth.

The Beachcomber

A Dream Poem

Why should I be bitter, rueful?
Pain can often be quite useful
to sharpen up the senses,
close in experience,
condense the mood,
and nurture purity,
that nucleus of good
alive within my being.

Why should I be bitter,
living as I do,
clinging to the few
brief moments,
friends and thoughts
that matter most?
Yet I know self-pity
as I roam these lonely shores
through scraps of tassled seaweed,
lazy refuse freed
by the night breeze,
sun-curled love-notes
drifting surreptitiously,
orange-peel, sweet-papers
cart-wheeling capriciously.

Why should I be bitter,
feeling as I do,
yearning for a new
sensation or experience:
love-enticing face,
moonshine on soft forms,
passionate embrace?

What if some day
I should chance to find
on a warm Aegean shore
a Grecian head
with perfect nose and candid eyes
and lips like Cupid's bow?
Shall I ever know such joy?
Then would old gods
cry into the stillness:
"Never mind that nothing moves,
since all revolves, improves."
For I am I
and do not ask for more
as I move on down this lonely shore.

Why should I be bitter,
going on alone,
collecting up the litter of my life
and so for life atone?

The Night Visitor

Through the lush savannas of my dreams
he creeps like a vampire,
leaps to my open window,
leans over me in the darkness,
eyelids rimmed with fire;
but dawn hounds him to his tomb
in the black crypt of my soul;
sunrise bursts through the leaves,
and fills the waking house with joy.

As With Iago

I am like a rich and fertile land
Sketched in the indelible palm of the hand
With lines of life and head and heart;
But fate steps in to play the part
Iago feigned, when he betrayed
Othello for a handkerchief, strayed
Into those icy realms of fate
Where love puts on the mask of hate.

Some minor modulation moves
My thoughts to sacrifice, and proves
That kneeling calculations dwell
In the draughty corridors of hell,
Where hands stretch out and beg for alms,
And a hooded monk my heart embalms
And salts my savage wound, the crutch
Of life, the continent of touch.

Beware my heart, beware my head,
Beware things known, and things not said,
Beware my progress and redemption,
For, from death there's no exemption.
I know from self there's no escape,
And love takes many a form and shape;
To suffer eternity on the rack
Would be, like Donne, to "walk in black."

There is no wealth this world could share
(Outside its suffering and despair)
To match the love that humankind
Could bring to bear (if it had the mind)
On every circumstance of life,
Whether man or lover, child or wife.
I know this power, in every nerve.
Make firm this faith my life must serve.

In These Places…
…At These Times
1952-71

Mistral Sound

Cannes, 1953

Horizons fade beyond the summer haze,
As rose rocks glide into the sea,
All purpled by the seaweed green
Of deep windless waters slipping to the sands.
The ancient castle sleeps in misting leaf
Above the harbour, where gaunt masts
Needle to the unencumbered sky; and over all,
The soothing rays of Riviera sun.

Then, sudden, in the night, the north wind strikes
Against the sinister and black and flashing eyes
Of Algerines who flaunt the quays
And sound the beaches with their sugared cries.
The blustering winds of the Mistral blow
And spiral up the sands to stinging cheeks;
White horses somersault across the bay,
While swaying palms decline, incline, decline
In angered repetition at the gusts, which,
Out at sea, make white sails billow in urgent task
Towards the Château of the Iron Mask.

This rush of sound: the whistling of the wind,
The crunching of the yachts against the quay,
The crashing of the waves upon the rocks,
The shouting of the fishermen to heave
The seething nets and turn about to lee:
There's pride of nature in this Mistral sound.

Out at Honorat, towards the open water,
Where seeds of sycamore whisk into the waves
And an avenue of eucalyptus shades
The tired eyes from the persuasive sun,
Monks meditate amid the noise of nature;
Their language is the silence of the soul
And brings a peace which only they can know
Where the winds of the Mistral blow.

For Usana

Le Château de l'Isle–
La Sarthe, 1956

The Château Fort de l'Isle was given by Henry V to Lancelot de l'Isle, who was eventually killed at the Siege of Orleans.

This ruined chapel, overgrown
  With alder bushes, on the hill
Two crumbling towers of sepia stone
  Were once a castle by the mill.

Down in the dungeon's eerie gloom
  A smell of death creeps from the clay;
Beyond the walls, wild roses bloom
  Beside a pleasant stream. Distrait,

Ophelia might have roamed these weeds,
  Where currents lace and intertwine
Through water-lilies, tangled reeds,
  Among the apple and the vine.

And down between the trailing threads,
  The gleaming sheen of steel-blue perch,
Through mingled yellows, greens and reds,
  Dart nervously in constant search

For water-flies, whilst water-rats,
  Basking on wads of autumn leaves,
Straddle after whining gnats
  Down by the weir. Below the eaves,

The broken wheel is stilled with time;
  No swallows swoop in field or lane;
On banks of moss, in woods of pine,
  Warm summers blush and fade again.

This ruined chapel, dark and lone,
  These alder bushes by the mill,
These crumbling towers of sepia stone
  Now lie forlorn, and dank, and still.

To Oleg Kerensky

On Seeing Pasternak's "Doctor Zhivago"
London, 1958

London. Late evening. Leicester Square.
A one-man bandsman limps along the queue,
jarring our senses with his reckless noise.
"Pay up!" we think. "Be quick! Anything for peace."
"Peace!" we wonder … "Where is peace?"
Under the dark trees, Shakespeare ponders
advertisements for every kind of pleasure.
Garish colours glisten through the rain.
A young girl croons the theme of Pasternak's "Zhivago"
below the drumming din of the band's insane farrago.

At last, we enter plastic marble halls,
spring over thick carpets of artificial weave,
to buy our candies, fumble for our seats.
In hush of darkened auditorium, the city
vanishes. Fresh images of an unfamiliar past
absorb our willing minds, mysteriously moulding
all we know and all we are to know
in the malleable shapes of scenic fantasies:

Leaves, like locusts, flood the plains;
an old man comes with messages of peace;
in a Moscow street, a Cossack sabre
stains the gutter with a peasant's blood.
News comes that they have shot the Czar
and all his family. When will it cease?

Far from the rage of Moscow fires,
boy-soldiers stalk with untried guns
through the ungathered sheaves of corn,
boys in boots too big for boys their age:
partisans crouch in the knotted briars,
their gunfire spatters the stubble with young blood.
Here, in the Urals at least, Russia will not change,
though the earth is scorched with death.

Far from the city's impassioned insurrection,
black minarets of home stand in the shining snow;
in the breeze, a chandelier chinks and chimes;
through a torn roof, snowflakes gently fall
onto an old familiar desk, and poems flow.
No use pretending. The killing is not over,
though love will conquer if Lara is the theme.

Where are the old men with their talk of peace?
New men will not listen to a poet's voice;
old images are shorn of sense, outgrown:
the best sentence in the language is hard labour.
How Voltaire would have grinned at the fun!
All over Russia, bolsheviks chant in unison,
link arms and dance, salute the people's flag.

In the Urals, at least the seasons will not change:
snowflakes will softly fall, poems germinate and grow,
new hopes will breed, memories shall not die,
though winters will be lonely — like a shroud
for those who dare to think their thoughts aloud ...

Theme music reverberates through the mind.
The lights go up; the garish glare returns.
Thus ending, a troubled peace prevails,
as over plastic cups and patinas of ash
we trample the specious magic of the screen.

London. Early morning. Leicester Square.
The busker beats his drums to squeeze our pockets dry.
"Peace!" we think. "What, where, oh when is peace?"
Reluctant, we loiter for a moment in the rain,
scan early editions of the Sunday papers
for the usual catalogue of violence and greed,
hijack a taxi-driver bent on going East,
tease him with fancy tips, bludgeon him with words.
In the rain, we too begin to haggle and protest.
So, homeward to Kensington, in the "golden" West!

"The party's over." "Farewell Leicester Square."
"Goodbye Piccadilly." — Images, threadbare.
No use pretending love will conquer here.
No new men lead us with a poet's voice,
no raging of fires, no messages of peace.
Yet, listen! Out of the dawning of our discontent,
out of fragmented images of bloodshed and of snow,
poems, like love, or happiness, germinate and grow.

"Romantic Ireland's dead and gone"

*W. B. Yeats' words, remembered at his graveside
on the 20th anniversary of his death.
Sligo, 1959*

Gone is that once-contented land
    Where joy and pleasure reigned,
Where love and youth went hand-in-hand
    And virtue was unstained.

Gone are the gardens of the mind,
    Gone is the thrust of life,
Dead his youth and dead his love,
    Usurped by age and strife.

Gone are the pleasures of this world;
    His destiny is a stone;
He lies in the moss of his ancient land,
    Cold, restless, and alone.

To a Dolphin
Brittany, 1959

I remember a dolphin
Caught off the Breton shores
As she soared and glided through the spray
On her way to the torrid Azores.

The fisherfolk huddled around her,
As she gasped on the gleaming strand;
They waited, so silent, to see her
Breathe her last on the streaming sand.

Her back was a turmoil of colour
From violet to yellow and red,
Black was her beauty, yet dying,
Shone like a rainbow when she lay dead.

I dream of that gleaming dolphin
Riding on crests of white horses,
Leaping through spray across the bay
As she soars and capriols and courses.

My ship is so small on the waters,
Its burden so frail and so light,
The ocean so hungry for mourning
As I battle to keep her in sight.

O how I long, shining dolphin,
To see you again in your prime,
To ride you astride on the ocean,
To lose all remembrance of time.

My feet are entombed in the white sand;
O how I long to be free.
O answer my innermost yearning:
Will I die in a rainbow sea?

You followed me once, graceful dolphin;
O follow once more to the cool
Waters of the gleaming white islands,
To my silver and amethyst pool.

Fireflies

Rila Mountains, Bulgaria, 1961

Down from the mountain's melting snows,
I sought the dark and lonely way.
They whispered, "See, see, there goes
The dreamer who longs for the dawn."
But their voices were only the cries of birds,
And my path was strewn with thorn.

Into the forest's enchanted night,
I crept like a frightened child,
Deeper I crept, and deeper still —
My fear was the fear of the grave.
A sadness came over me like a veil
In that dark and mysterious glade.

For hour upon hour I slept and dreamed,
Awoke to find amidst the trees
Fireflies, flooding my glade with light,
Haloes of phosphorus in silver-green night,
Fluttering, glittering comets of gold,
A myriad of stars among the leaves.

The vision vanished at dawn, and then
Day lifted me up to a golden sky.
I saw that my life was changed by the sight
To a wonder of joy and a wonder of light.
I walked in the sun with my head held high,
At one with the world, at peace again.

My way is strewn with the flowers of the earth,
The vision an image in memory now.
From boyhood to manhood, from birth to rebirth,
I seek out the dazzling fireflies' way,
As they whisper softly, "See who goes there!
The voyager of the bright day."

Ballad of Mea She'arim
Jerusalem, 1962

The Sabbath Day is a dangerous day
In the Orthodox part of the city;
Wise children never go out to play
On a day when there's no pity.

A Christian climbed to Mea She'arim,
His camera poised to record;
They smashed it to pieces at his feet
And jeered at his "gentle Lord".

A kindly Jew in an invalid-car
Crept slowly over the hill;
With sticks and stones they left their scar;
I remember his screaming still.

The Sabbath Day is a dangerous day
In the Orthodox part of the city;
Wise children never go out to play
On a day when there's no pity.

Scorpion
Tel Aviv, 1962

Black and white marble squares.
She stood barefoot on the white.
I lingered breathless by the stairs.
Her face was pale with fright.

Scorpion roused on a square of black,
Poised to strike, tail arched.
We stared at its brittle scaly back,
Her lips were strained and parched.

Back in the Desert War, for a fling,
When we were bored or tight,
We put two scorpions in a ring
Of petrol and watched them fight.

When one had struck the other dead,
It struck itself the same;
We watched it writhe from tail to head
In the dying petrol flame.

My boot came down. She gave a cry.
How easily death scares!
But I still remember the barefooted girl
On the black and white marble squares.

Biafra Poems
Christmas Television, 1968

1. Lament of an Ibo Warrior for his Dead Son

Away from the silent sea,
Far from Fernando Po,
Under the cool plane tree,
Death has dealt its blow.

Was it painful when you perished?
Did they wound you with torturing threat?
Was it hunger or fear that killed you?
Was it shrapnel, or bayonet?

In the lines, with the wounded and dying,
Know that I never lost heart.
Can you forgive me for fighting
For a cause that was lost from the start?

I am blinded by my old hatreds,
You are free in a world unknown;
When I die, you will not be here to defend
The fruit of the seeds I have sown.

Away from the silent sea,
Death has dealt its blow,
Under the cool plane tree,
Far from Fernando Po.

2. Biafran Child on Christmas Day

Defenceless child, you squat there
on the ground,
your tiny limbs
no thicker than a bird's;
your tearful eyes
accuse us
with bewildered stare.

We who snuggle warm
in our comfortable chairs —
are we responsible?
The hurt came
when you smiled into the camera
and reconciled our pity
with your forgiveness.

Business Train

Essex, 7th August, 1971

For my part, I want to scream.

Squeezed from overcrowded compartments
into sweat-lined corridors, I am wedged
tight between barricades of glass.
Somnolent typists and tired clerks wilt.
A sleek-haired man in pin-stripe,
slumped in his comfortable first-class seat,
casts a weary eye over his documents,
his face red as a geranium.
Amidst the flurry and crackle of newspapers,
his quietly-elegant personal assistant
discreetly fingers her hair
and daintily sips her gin and tonic.

Speeding like this through the dingy suburbs,
only the train shows any real signs of movement.
No-one bothers with the summer sky,
brilliant aquamarine through clouds crimson and flame
below deepening blue of evening.

What miracle is this that fails to give life
to the motionless figures in the corridors?
What miracle that does not draw eyes from newspapers
on this momentous evening, in this
the warmest of never-to-be-forgotten summers?

For my part, I want to scream.

Instead, I write in my notebook:
"Far beyond the jostling of the city,
far beyond the unnoticed clouds,
over the white horizons of the moon,
men are walking in space.
They, like us, are journeying towards home."

The train whistles through a station,
plunges into the last of our tunnels.
No-one stirs in these corridors of the dead.
No amiable stars twinkle welcome.
No crimson loveliness lingers over our familiar fields.
Deliberately, as of habit, robots silently prepare
to alight at the next stop, briefcases
Filled with the usual apathy.
Then the sudden screech of brakes.
Darkness is all that remains,
and the long, long days ahead.

For my part, I want to scream

House Mouse

Holland Street, Kensington, 1972

At the edge of the carpet
a small brown shadow
flickered for an instant
and was gone. It was comic!
Was that vodka too atomic?
Perhaps the pâté was too rich.
(The liver plays wicked games
with the innocence of eyes!)
Whatever it was, or might have been,
the edge of the carpet could be seen
to have all the appearance of being —
the edge of the carpet!
A minuscule brown ball of fluff
hovered for a moment like a tiny puff
of smoke from a toy electric train.
Then — squeak! squeak!
Hop, skip, and scamper,
four little feet
nimbly manoeuvre in balletic style
enormous palisades of pile.

Clumsily, I — a grim, gigantic ogre —
clamber over the mountainous sofa,
maraud the territory
like a hideous brontosaurus
to terrify a prey so frail —
no longer than my thumb
if you include his tail —
round and plump as a suede button.
Grasping a saucepan in my hand,
I jump, I leap, I crouch, I stand,
I pounce, I strike — and, limp,
I trap this cowering and yet cheeky imp.

The memory of his mangled corpse,
crushed to a pulp of blood and bone,
will *not* haunt me
as I free him under the lilac-tree,
see him scurry through my neighbour's door,
whilst I, gaping in the street,
contemplate my saucepan, emptied now
of those pattering
metallic-sounding tiny feet.

Today — he came back. No attempt to hide.
Up the curtain, across the pelmet,
down the other side.
Hop, skip, scamper, squeak!
He makes me feel so vexed.
You see, there is no telling
when he will come again
or *what* he will do next!

Trappists

The Flea Catcher

Hampstead Heath, London, 1973

"They feed on human blood," he said,
happily rolling up his shirt-sleeve.
The flea punctured the skin, delicately,
leaving a tiny speck of red.
"I'd give a pound a dozen to anyone,
only, few people ever admit to having 'em.
That's the reason for the shortage.

"There's no end to the varieties:
some walk the tight-rope,
some carry things,
some hop — they're the ballet-dancers.
A catcher has to cosset 'em for the circus,
find out the potential,
discover their talents.

"It's that harnessing that's tricky,
passing the hair-fine wire under the hind legs.
Great little jumpers, they are!
The occasional one a regular genius,
if you're lucky not to snap 'is legs off in the wire.
Killed hundreds at first ...
Know anyone with a nice hedgehog?"

He rolled down his sleeve,
covering twenty tiny specks of blood.
"Most of 'em live only a few days," he said sadly.
"Some maybe up to a fortnight.
The secret is:
find their talents, train 'em quick ...
specially the ballet-dancers.
Poor little bleeders!"

In Lighter Vein

Picture Poem: *Strawberry Hill*

Picture Poem: *Stepping out of Line*

A Flying Visit

A firefly wisped in at my window
   One sultry summer's night,
I was searching for my slippers,
   So I asked her for a light.
And what do you think she answered,
   As she glittered like a jewel?
"I can't stay long, my darling one!
   I'm running short of fuel!"

Lines to an Astronaut

Do not take water to the moon;
Beneath the dust the rock is porous.
Who can tell what hideous things
Old H_2O could spread before us?

Things that follow in our traces,
Poisonous, sluggish grey balloons,
With sticky feet and oozing faces —
Even H. G. Wells would swoon.

Please don't take water to the moon,
However spacemen may deplore us;
We might discover all too soon
Another deadly dinosaurus.

Something at the Foot of the Bed!

Of all the hateful beasties
   I hope I never meet,
The serpent not the least is,
   Because he has no feet.

O he'll make me, yes, he'll will me
   To soon put out the light,
Then he'll slither up and kill me
   With a serpentine delight.

He'll curl up at the bottom
   Of my warm and cuddly bed;
O my toes! I know he'll knot 'em
   Up and bite 'em till they're red.

I think I'll turn the blankets back
   To see if he's in sight;
No, there's nothing, not a trace or track.
   O well! I'll say: "Goodnight!"

A Social Menace–

Who was it chose
The rhinoceros's toes
And those eyes so puny and sad?
  Lumbering,
  Clumbering,
  In the mud slumbering,
He's O, such a wily old cad.

One moment he's mellow,
Then he lets out a bellow,
Kicks up such a shindy-din-din;
  Snuffling,
  Scuffling,
  He's hopeless at muffling
The clack of his hard, plated skin.

He's O, so ferocious,
So bumptious, precocious,
His fury is really a farce;
  Snorting,
  Cavorting,
  And all that hog-warting,
My dear! on a diet of grass!

Press Gang

Our planet's beset by a dangerous plight,
With its nations all grabbing (for wrong or for right),
While cant correspondents spread doom and despondence,
And the media relish in violence and spite.

The world loves to read a sensational press,
A scandal, a plane crash, some marital stress,
A rape or a murder, a blow on the head,
"Hurricane strikes with hundreds of dead!"

Oil-tankers aground and North Sea pollution,
Middle East 'Peace Talks' with no real solution.
Crime on the increase, a fire on the Ferry,
A flooding in India, insurrection in Derry.

The dearth of compassion one everywhere finds,
Shows the media is set upon stealing our minds.
My birthday's tomorrow; there's one present I'd like:
To hear, in the morning, the Press are on strike!

P. Thorogood
1975

Picture Poem: *The Secret of the Loch!*

Nessiteras Rhombopteryx, or, *Monster Hoax by Sir Peter S.*

The Bachelor

O it's lager for Sue, and beer for Sal,
Gin for Kate and vodka for Mandy,
Deirdre likes a good Beaujolais,
But I'm looking for a girl to share my shandy.

I'm the man who fancies himself,
A bit of a wag, a bit of a dandy,
The slimline shirt, the snazzy tie,
And a stock by the bed of chocs and candy.

I'm the man in the crowded bar,
A little too plump, a little too trendy,
But not half so *wet*, not nearly so *soppy*
As that *drip* in the corner chatting up Wendy.

I'm the man who is "over forty",
So available, so handy
For any nice girl who wouldn't mind a chap
That's not too poor and not too randy.

So it's lager with Sue, and beer with Sal,
Gin with Kate and vodka with Mandy,
Deirdre likes a good Beaujolais,
But I'm looking for a girl to share my shandy.

On second thoughts:

There's Brenda and Mary and Trudie and Dolly
And Sandra and Sarah and Megan and Molly
And Janet and Lizzie and Barbara and Polly
And Hedda and Helga and Hattie and Holly;
There's Caroline, too, but she needs some persuasion —
Look, I'll tell you the rest on some other occasion!

A Hypochondriac to his G.P.

Prescribe lotions and pills
As a cure for my ills,
And a short sharpish shock for my hiccup;
Some linctus and plasters
(In case of disasters)
And a tonic to give me a peck-up.
Dear Doctor, do give me a check-up.

Please tell me, dear Doctor,
Now, can you concoct a
Nice medicine to cure all of these!
I'm so down in the dumps;
Is it measles? or mumps?
Is it love? — like the birds and the bees?
Or some far more deadly disease?

Is it gout? Is it cancer?
Am I just a romancer?
It is *pain*fully clear I'm a pain!
Is it *quad*ruple *quin*sy?
An attack of the Kinsey?
Do tell me, dear Doctor, again!
Is it housemaid's knee — on the brain?
Do tell me, dear Doctor, again!

Picture Poem: *One-Way Street*

For Joyce Grenfell

Tea-Time Recital

Reader: *O Beauteous stream ...*

Mabel: ... It's best Ceylon!

Reader: *I love thee still.*

Mabel: ... er — weak or strong?

Reader: *Dost thou glide on to distant seas ...*

Mabel: The sandwiches are jam or cheese!

Reader: *Alone, through forests, undismayed?*

Alice: I'll take the jam. Is it homemade?

Reader: *Thy snowy images of swans ...*

Mabel: Now, how's your cup? Do have some scones!

Reader: *Cool-mirrored in the silver sheen,*
Go gracefully, and slowly preen ...

Mabel: Have a cream puff! A little more jam?
So pleased you came. I really *am*!

Reader: *... and slowly preen*
Their dainty plumage to the moon.

Mabel: I think you need a larger spoon!

Reader: *Thou flowest to the ocean's brim ...*

Mabel: More cream, my dear? You're still *quite* slim!

Reader: *Eternally, while woodlands mourn*
The passing day to darkness drawn.

Alice: Delicious chocolate gâteau, too!
I *do* love poetry, don't you?

Split Personality

I'm very like the spry Ducrow,
That famous London circus beau,
Who, nightly, before astonished eyes,
Bestrode four horses in a row —
A kind of comic tour-de-force,
A man too agile for one horse.
Compared to his, my own conflicting talents —
To paint, compose, write poetry, do research —
On backs of muses strive to keep the balance,
Demand expression, struggle for a perch.

A roll of drums! A shout! "Strike up the band!"
I stand astride my horses, reins in hand,
Four sets at each exhilarating show,
And round the circus-ring of life I go,
My muses galloping and cavorting,
Foaming at the bit, noses snorting,
My talents adjusting to every tilt and lurch —
Now painting, now poetry, now music, now research —
I do it all in comic starts and fits.
I hope, like poor Ducrow, I shall not do the splits!

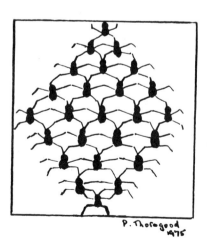

Picture Poem: *Fantastic Feet*

68

Under English Skies

1965-72

To Eve Moore

Ballad of the Singing Sands

For European Conservation Year 1970,
on the 200th anniversary of the birth of William Wordsworth

The curious 'singing sands' of the Hebrides make strange
music when trodden underfoot or blown by rough winds.

I dreamed of a land of singing sands,
Winnowed and washed by the restless seas,
The singing sands of the western isles,
On the shores of the golden Hebrides.

I deserted a land of poisoned cities,
A land where nature was scarred and torn,
A populous land of waste and litter,
A place of unrest and greed and scorn.

I passed by a land of potash mines,
As sere and bleak as a lonely fell;
No bird to be heard, no flower to be seen
In that stricken malevolent desert of hell.

I came to a land of lakes and mountains,
Of heather and gorse and forests of pine;
Woodlands alive with the beauty of bird-song,
The air was as clear as a vintage wine.

I heard on the moorlands, strange and haunting,
The glorious call of the whimbrel in spring;
Snow-bunting, ptarmigan, eagles from eyries
Over the mountaintops soared on the wing.

Behind was the land of teeming cities,
Beyond was the kingdom of murmuring seas,
Below were the sands with their siren-music,
On the shores of the golden Hebrides.

For Ursula Vaughan-Williams

The Memory Tree

An incident in the childhood of Ralph Vaughan-Williams

Old grandfather Cook
leaned back to gaze
at the tallest tree in England,
in Great Uncle Charles Darwin's way.
You, impish and boisterous,
longed to observe
the nature of the fall:
the splitting of the boughs,
the splintering of the trunk.
You screamed out ecstasy
over peaceful fields,
abruptly calling the men
from their sleep.
Respect the servants
and never tell tales,
or so your mother told you.
Gritting your teeth against
the rough edge of your life,
you remembered that falling trees
were dangerous to children.
Respect the servants ....
You wondered how it was
the cowman's wife had twins
coincidentally
on St. Valentine's Day!
Never ... tell ... tales ...
Old grandfather Cook
gazed down the long, straight
trunk of the silver-fir tree;
sighed as you laughed
at the stricken tree;
with the measure of age,
was saddened at this fracturing
of treasured things, this
brutal rearrangement
of the landscape.

God made the world in six days,
or so your mother told you.
Great Uncle Charles Darwin
thought it took centuries to grow
a tree as tall, as straight
and as proud, as a silver-fir tree.
Joy burst bitter on your tongue.
All the tree could do
was to go on growing
in your memory.

To Ralph Vaughan-Williams

Your baptism was as green as English trees;
you trod the upward and the downward path,
and, learning the pain and the pity of war,
you put out tendrils of hope.
Rough-hewn, as a great oak,
your leaves were jagged tunes
innocent as an old man's love;
your boughs wise as serpents.
In you, the tree of life was never quiet.
You made history from unrecorded song,
fashioned symphonies from the snows and seas.
In the dark forest, you did not flinch
where lemurs wrenched your roots
from the unrepentant earth.
Now, here, the gale blows high.
The wind in its old anger
shakes off the dust, and conquers time.

Summer Sea Fog
After Seurat

Hovering hungrily over horizon
Blurring the line of sea and sky
Blanketing wake of wary tankers
Holding up helmsmen coastward bound
Lazily gloomily fog-bank falling
Mysterious languid silent sly —
Lightsome the winds in lonely waters
Lively the yachts on bay and sound

Sea lanes (cool from winter solstice)
Warmed by soft winds up from south
Beaches stippled with bathers and boatmen
Laughter ripples sun and sea
Promenade strollers fading phantoms
Vanishing haven of river mouth
Fog-bank forming over coastline
Unsuspecting trippers flee —

Inland — hikers trek the valleys
Farmers till the sun-drenched soil
But coast is clammy — dank disaster
Looms the swirling cloud along
Rolling over beach and cliff-top
Billowing blending strand and coil
Suddenly silently darkening harbours
Muffling fog-horn's sombre song

Octopus creeping slily onward
Ghostly tentacles stifling pleasure —
Recognising signs and portents
Sailors and threshers strain their eyes
Picknickers pack up hamper and children —
Complaining of interrupted leisure
Discerning predetermined patterns
In our pale and treacherous skies

Sussex Downs above Worthing 1953

Tuscan Landscape near Siena 1954

The Hay Cart, Albyns Farm 1946

Harvest Time, Albyns Farm 1946

In Countryside Sleeping

October evenings
I remember best —
lazy smoke of bonfires
held close to earth,
seeping through sweetness
of garden smells,
vying with kitchen and farmyard.

Flat cirrus shapes
silver the setting sun.
Aroma of chaff and grain
hangs about barn and stable,
drifting up to windows
in soft breath of autumn.
Even fallen leaves are still.

Tarred roofs sink
sombre in half-light.
Pale orange orb of sun,
beyond wings of cloud,
sends shadows of saffron light
over green horizons.
A calm of evening is here.

Mist and smoke hug earth,
warning of frost. In the night,
wreaths of mist lie over fields,
writhing in furrow and ditch.
Though it is not yet dawn
in countryside sleeping,
the day will be most welcome.

I have seen those
who dwell in valleys
drown in a sea of mist,
and at morning whole villages
(submerged in the night)
rise again with the sun,
sparkling with hoar-frost.

"Look, we have come through!"

Bleak as the outlook may seem to us now
    when skies are crimson with morning
    and a deep depression settles over us

We should never be completely discouraged
    for high clouds thicken and break
    in banks over brilliant sunrise.

Making a good beginning is possible
    though light winds sweep over downland
    and gentle rain washes harbour and quay.

Some deception of wind and cloud is bound
    to alter the complexion of the sky
    and dampen our spirits at dawn astir.

An air of expectancy thrills early light:
    high stratus heaps itself up in the west
    and cirrus smoke-trails shred the sun;

For pilots have left signs in the sky, signs
    that yachtsmen must learn to read:
    as when rough gales threaten restless oceans.

Meaning is paramount in these portents;
    winds blow wintry over farm and field
    leaving next morning branches heavy with snow.

Bleak as the outlook may seem to us now
    whatever weather eventually comes should freshen
    lively these lovely landscapes of England.

Riviera Diary

1971

On Awaking with Bright Thoughts

Opening my eyes to the luminous morning,
I dwell on many pleasant things:
The *café-au-lait* and the crisp *croissants*
The pretty *femme-de-chambre* brings,

The cries of children on the beaches,
The welcome smell of fresh French loaves,
French coffee, soft ripe peaches,
Quiet picnics in deserted coves,

All these I dream in my comfortable bed —
Like swimming breast-stroke, and the crawl.
What pleasure there is in planning ahead —
Until I remember yesterday's fall!

I try to turn over, to sit up at least;
A pain shoots right up my arm and neck,
Sharp claws grip my throat like a ravenous beast —
I've fractured my arm! Oh! hell! Oh, heck!

Forget the quiet picnics, and games on the beaches,
Forget the French loaves and the soft ripe peaches,
Forget the damned holiday; — and what's really worse,
Forget the French maid! and call in the nurse!

Pigeon

High above the treacherous pavement
Where I slipped and painfully fell,
A scruffy pigeon cleans its feathers,
Perched on my fifth-floor window sill.

Clumsily, I descend the stairway,
Into the dread familiar street,
Cautiously guarding my plaster wing;
The dingy bird is there at my feet! —

Pecks at a crust, lifts off the ground,
Glides on a graceful arc of flight,
Leaving me rooted there, earthbound,
As I follow its scruffiness, on out of sight.

Out Walking with Myself

"Nous sommes sortis, tous les deux,
Moi avec moi" — Jacques Prévert

I am the well-presented man
pacing the evening promenade
sporting my raffish summer slacks
and voguish Dior tie and shirt
the man who modestly fancies himself
eyes the shapely sauntering girls
with their lovely contours of desire
and their voices softly calling him

I am the shy, deluded man
by far, too many years too old
trying to straddle the black abyss
between having — and not having —
competing with handsome youths from the town
in fitting T-shirts and blue jeans
who regularly tempt the girls
their voices softly calling them

I am the loved yet lonesome man
gazing over the taciturn sea
throwing the stray ball back to the children
dining alone at my separate table
the man who strums old tunes at the piano
there in the empty hotel lounge —
lie awake all night in my double-bed
dream-voices softly calling me

I am the quiet and kindly man
loitering lonely in crowded bars
remote from passion's pleasure now
observing the human comedy pass
the man who keeps himself to himself
at peace with these *enfants du paradis*
with their lovely contours of desire
and their voices softly calling me.

Bastinado

Next door to the Hotel Pacific
a woman is screaming from her window.

Through the slats of the shutters
we can see a man beating her
with his rough bony hands.

Though her screams tell a thousand stories,
her words are meaningless.

At the café in the street below,
another man, another woman,
quietly chew at their steaks.

The woman pours vinegar on the salad,
the man spreads mustard on the rare meat.

At the dingy, dimly-lit hotel,
two young lovers
play out their silent game of chess.

Yet nothing and everything
is explained here:

the screaming woman, the vinegar,
the bony hands,
the lovers at their game,

the darkened shutters
with their half-shared secrets.

Nothing echoes now along the lonely street,
only the voice of the passionate man,
the hungry man, and the silent woman weeping.

Le Dessert

Under the table with the check cloth,
A poodle whined with prurient pleasure.
A woman with brightly-painted cheeks
Was reclining there at her leisure.

And cooing and purring and smiling there,
She leaned to stroke her darling:
"O comme il est doux, O comme il est beau!"
(He was black as a black male starling.)

She stroked her neighbour's manly knee;
He impassively picked at his teeth,
And gazed into space with a look on his face —
Well! she was touching him — underneath!

The glasses chinked, the table shook,
The poodle whimpered with pleasure,
And the woman petted the manly knee,
And patted the dog for good measure!

"O comme il est bon, O comme il est fou,
O comme il est mon chéri!" she sighed,
"O comme il est beau, O comme il est doux!"
The eyes of the manly man opened wide.

And all the while she was stroking and petting,
He impassively picked at his teeth,
And gazed into space with a look on his face,
While she fondled him — underneath!

The poodle came up from under the table
And licked her open hand,
And the heart of the man burst out into song,
Loud as trumpets in a brass band.

He paid up the bill; the meal was concluded;
The woman's smile was like honey.
He patted the dog, threw down on the table
A thousand francs in good money.

"O comme il est bon, O comme il est fou,
O comme il est mon chéri," she cried.
"O comme il est beau, O comme il est doux! —
Mais comme il est si avare!" she sighed.

She watched him slip quietly into the darkness,
Picked up her lipstick and picked up her pay,
Picked up her poodle and picked up her handbag —
And picked up a man in a Chevrolet!

In These Places, At These Times

The wind comes caressing the silent shore,
soothing the sinews of the drowsy town,
bearing tales of dark ancestral lands.

In these places, at these times, we sense
the veiled embraces of the hidden self.

The lighthouse rises to a crown of fire
out of the shimmering loins of the sea,
flooding the darkness in jets of white light.

The dark flank of the mountain over the bay
cleaves the red horns of the wandering moon.

Larches lean from dark-descending cliffs,
like gibbets in the blood-red noose of dawn,
branches, the lifeless limbs of dreams long dead.

Dinosaurus-headland sleeping sound
under the drooping horns of the moon.

Yet, now, the moment of ecstasy has passed,
and even the mountain (still to climb)
as soon sinks in a floating veil of mist.

In these places, at these times, we learn
the secret emblems of the wheeling stars.

We see, in this reflected image of our hopes,
a wilderness to wake and wander through
before each day is asked for and enjoyed.

About the Author

Peter Thorogood was born on 2nd June 1927 at Albyns Farm, Hornchurch, Essex. He was educated at Brentwood School, where, besides developing a keen interest in history, classics and English literature, he took up painting in watercolours, and became proficient in musical composition. His early achievements were comparatively modest, winning a class prize for parody of Longfellow, and composing a suite of incidental music for the School production of Shakespeare's *The Tempest*. On leaving school in 1946, he entered the London School of Economics, where his tutor was Harold Laski. He continued his musical studies at the Guildhall School of Music, transferring to the Royal Irish Academy of Music after he was offered a place at Trinity College, Dublin to read Modern Languages.

On his graduation in 1952, Peter went to Italy to teach English as a foreign language. At that time, the fashion for learning English was increasing, and Peter began to develop ideas for his highly successful course on the history of English Literature, and a special short course on English Pronunciation by means of simplified phonetics, courses which he continued to promote on his return to England under the auspices of the British Council and, later, as a senior lecturer in English at the Polytechnic of Central London. At this time (1958), Peter was beginning to write more poetry and, over the next ten years, published several volumes of his work, which included, not only his poetry, but a volume of comic verse, illustrated with his own comic pen-and-ink sketches.

Soon, he was organising recitals of poetry and music, reading his own work and playing his own music, with performances at the City Literary Institute (with the writer, Clemence Dane), the Highgate Literary Institution, the Chelsea Poetry Circle, and other venues. His comic verse was first performed by John Stuart Anderson for the Dulwich Poetry Group in 1961. His poetry and music were performed by Joan Murray Simpson and Alan Wheatley at Holland House Kensington in 1973. A performance of his work was given in the Music Room of his home, St. Mary's Bramber on the occasion of his 60th birthday, by Gwyneth Powell, Alan Leith, Thalia Myers (piano) and Helen Arnold (harp).

Among his other activities, Peter Thorogood was Radio Talks Critic for the BBC publication, *The Listener*, appeared regularly on the BBC Radio Two series 'Your Verdict', with veteran broadcaster, John Snagge, and compiled a series on 'English Humorous Writing' for the BBC World Service. He is also an authority on the life and work of the Victorian poet and caricaturist, Thomas Hood, and has delivered a number of scholarly papers on the subject at King's College and University College, London. Recently, his songs, piano music, guitar music, and music for violin and piano have been recorded by Neil Jenkins (tenor), Terence Allbright (piano), Richard Storry (guitar) and Tim Callaghan (violin). The publication of *In These Places, At These Times* by the Bramber Press celebrates Peter Thorogood's 70th birthday.